SWEET SUE'S ADVENTURES

Sweet Sue's Adventures

Story by SAM CAMPBELL

Photographs by CHARLES PHILIP FOX

the NEW *Bobbs-Merrill* COMPANY, INC.

AN ASSOCIATE OF HOWARD W. SAMS & CO., INC.

Publishers • INDIANAPOLIS • NEW YORK

SWEET SUE'S ADVENTURES
is a realistic story about a mother
skunk and her eight baby skunklets.

CONTENTS

SWEET SUE'S ADVENTURES

Our
First Hike

COME! We are going on a hike across the countryside! We shall see what kind of adventure we can find, so close to home that we are almost in our own back yard. Take your camera, a book in which to make notes of what we see and a pair of binoculars. A small flashlight often comes in handy on a nature hike, too.

Today is a lovely day. Gentle winds make the new leaves dance. The air hums with the soft voices of insects and birds. In the world of nature, wonderful things are happening. We do not want to miss anything. Let's go walking in the oldest and best playground of all—the outdoors.

We wander through fields and groves that surround a small country village. Most of what we see is farm land, where the food we eat is growing. A farmer is working in his field. He looks strong, healthy and happy. Farming is fun, but a great amount of work, too.

How many animals are on his farm? Look over in the pasture. There are cows, horses and sheep. In a pen near the barn there are several pigs. Chickens peck while they walk about their pen, feeding. A large brown dog sits near the farmhouse. He barks at us several times, which is probably his way of saying, "Hello, you're welcome to come in, but don't do any damage to my farm." A farm would not be complete without a dog.

Near the barn, a cat moves along in the

silent way which is natural for a cat. No doubt it is her duty to keep the farm free of mice and rats.

These are domestic animals we see, the animals that have learned to live with people. But there are other kinds, too, right on this very land. Many wild creatures live out in the deep grasses, along hedges, in the groves of trees and in brush thickets.

"What kind would be here?" you ask.

Well, it could be that right in this country before us there are foxes, woodchucks, gophers, chipmunks, squirrels, skunks, coyotes and many kinds of birds.

"May we see them?" you ask.

Yes, but to see wild animals we must be quiet and patient. See that grove of trees just beyond the garden? Let's walk over there and see what we can find.

It is thrilling to go searching in the outdoors. Anything can happen. We watch carefully as we go along. There goes a chipmunk bouncing along as if he were a rubber ball! He disappears into his home, which is a hole in the ground. How cute he is! Now a big woodchuck who has been watching us whistles a warning and then disappears into the ground. How quick and alert wild creatures are! The flute-like song of a wood thrush floats out of the grove before us. We pause to listen. This is one of the most beautiful bird songs in the world.

Now another sound comes to us. What is it, and where is it? It comes from a place where a large decayed log lies on the ground. Scratch, scratch, scratch. We look at each other puzzled. What could it be? We move forward cautiously the way Indians travel. We are careful not to step on a twig or to crush leaves.

"There he is!" you whisper excitedly.

Yes, there he is—an animal about the size

of a large house cat. One look, though, and
we know it is not a cat. No, he has a long
nose. Cats have short noses. The animal be-
before us has a white line between his eyes.
There are two long white stripes which run
the length of his back.

While we watch, the creature scratches
again at the decaying log. He uncovers a
white grubworm. He eats it down—then
another, and another. How he enjoys his
delicious meal!

"Ugh!" you say, wrinkling your nose.

No, you wouldn't like those worms, but to the animal on the log they are choice tidbits.

What is that creature we watch? You know. Yes, it is a striped skunk, one of the most useful and friendly animals of the American countryside.

Did you ever see a skunk before? Some people have not. Yet there are many skunks throughout most of our land. Not all of them are the striped skunks. There are other kinds. The little spotted skunk is found in the southeastern part of our country. The hognosed skunk lives in the Southwest. The hooded skunk lives in Mexico.

However, the striped skunk is more numerous. Scientists call him *Mephitis mephitis*. The Latin word *mephitis* means "a poison gas." You can understand why that is true. An Indian name for him is *shee*

17

gawk. Some historians think the name Chicago was taken from this Indian word.

"Why don't we smell this one?" you ask. "Doesn't a skunk stink?"

Yes, sometimes he does, but not always. The odor of the skunk is his defense. He does not use it unless he thinks something is going to harm him. When he does use the odor, it is awful. Everyone in the whole region knows a skunk is around.

How does he do it? Well, you have probably seen a perfume bottle with a bulb attached. When you squeeze the bulb it sprays perfume. The skunk has a bulb at the base of his tail. When he is frightened, he squeezes it with his muscles. What comes out is not perfume! It is a yellow liquid and mist that burns the eyes and hurts the nostrils of any creature it touches.

Oh! Oh! The farm dog is coming this way. He has seen the skunk, too. He does not welcome the creature on his farm. He certainly looks cross, and he growls a challenge.

"Look out there, Rover!" the farmer calls, looking up from his work. "You'll get in a heap of trouble there. That little fellow won't hurt you if you let him alone. In fact, a skunk is valuable around this farm."

But Rover does not hear his master's warning. He is too concerned about that two-striped animal. Maybe he thinks it is a cat. He has chased many cats, and he likes to see them run and climb trees. He tries to chase this one, but it will not chase! It just stands there and faces him.

The dog does not know that the skunk is giving him three warnings. Skunks usually do. They are never anxious to start trouble. Their attitude is "Let me alone and I'll let you alone."

Notice the warnings. First the skunk

chatters his teeth. If Rover were a wise dog, he would turn back now. But he is not very smart, and he walks toward the skunk, growling and barking.

Now the skunk stiffens his body and beats

the ground with his front feet. That is the second warning. Still Rover comes on, probably wondering, "Why doesn't that crazy cat run?" Next the skunk raises his tail! This is the last warning.

"Rover!" calls the farmer, in alarm.

"Rover!" we echo, feeling very helpless.

The dog does not pay attention to us. He walks right on toward a calamity.

The skunk has given all his warnings now, and he is ready for battle. His bead-like eyes watch the dog fearlessly. His legs are stiff, and his tail is held high. He has great confidence in his ability to defend himself.

The skunk seems to have the same battle cry heard at Bunker Hill, "Fire when you see the whites of their eyes." Rover is now ten feet from the skunk. This is target range, and our striped friend goes into action. His moves are so swift that we can scarcely fol-

low them with our eyes. He does not turn his rear end toward the enemy. He does not need to, for he can spray in any direction without moving his front feet. Now he lifts his back feet off the ground and swings his body so it is shaped like the letter U. At the same time the muscles under his tail contract and squeeze the bulb.

Poor Rover! A thin yellow spray strikes him in the face. In an instant he is in more misery than he ever imagined possible. He jumps in the air. He howls mournfully. He rolls on the ground "sick as a dog," and paws at his burning eyes. Faster than we can tell it, the battle is over, and Rover is utterly defeated.

The farmer walks over to us. He looks at the miserable Rover and shakes his head. "You foolish dog," he says. "Why didn't you listen when we called to you? Why didn't you mind your own business and let that ani-

mal alone? Why didn't you heed the warnings of the skunk? Look at you now! I'll wash you and wash you, but you'll smell terrible just the same. You can't come in the house for days."

But Rover is not listening. He has faced an animal that has some of the best defenses in the world, and he came out second best.

The air is filled with the pungent odor. We hold our noses and walk away.

You ask, "Where is the skunk?"

He goes back through the woods slowly. Strangely enough, this animal never soils his own fur when he sprays. He is not mad at anyone. He will not go far. Skunks never do. They can live in rather small areas and be perfectly happy.

We watch this little creature for a moment. Now we see it more closely and realize it is a mother skunk. This is the time of year when she will have babies, and she is looking for a home. She searches in the brush. She crawls in and out of a hollow tree. She finds an opening in an old stump near a stone wall and disappears. Perhaps the hollow in the stump was the home of a fox. Skunks often take over a deserted fox den.

When we look around, we see that this would be a nice neighborhood for this skunk to live in. She can feed on worms and lizards which will crawl along that old stone wall. Out in the tall grasses of the near-by meadow are field mice, grasshoppers and other insects she likes to eat. There is a pond just over a low ridge. She can drink here, and catch frogs and little swimming creatures. Yes, this is a good place for a skunk to live.

Look, look! She is sticking her nose out of the opening. See how contented she is. She has decided this place is to be her new home. Wonderful! We can come to this spot again and see her, and maybe we will see her family, too.

Do you think we should give her a name? What do you suggest? Stinker? I think we can do better than that. Remember, she did not want to spray that dog. She does not smell bad most of the time.

Try another name, please. Sweet Sue? That sounds better. Sweet Sue it is. We will hike back to see her many times in the days to come.

What have we learned on our first hike? Let's make a list.

1. The two-striped skunk is about the size of a large cat.

2. He is dark, almost black in color, and has two long stripes down his back and a white line between his eyes.

3. He claws decayed logs and eats bugs and worms he finds there.

4. He does not use his defensive odor unless he is attacked.

5. His odor sack is under his tail, and it operates something like a perfume bulb. The skunk's muscles around the sack contract, and a yellow spray comes out.

6. He can shoot his spray about ten feet in any direction. He does not have to turn his back toward his enemy.

7. He gives three warnings before he sprays: First, he chatters his teeth. Then he beats the ground with his front feet. Finally he raises his tail.

8. His home is in hollows or burroughs under the ground. Sometimes he lives in dens that have been made by foxes or other animals.

9. He does not soil his own fur when he sprays.

Our
Second Hike

IT IS DAWN. The long rays of the sun tint the morning clouds pink. It is a wonderful time for a walk in nature. The world seems fresh and new. Shall we go to the grove where we last saw Sweet Sue and see if she likes her home? Bring the camera, field glasses, notebook and a small flashlight. Let's be off!

Notice that the meadows look as if they were set with jewels. Dew drops cling to the grasses and sparkle like diamonds when they are touched by the sun rays. Our shoes become wet quickly as we wade along.

Listen to the chorus of birds as they sing a greeting to the dawn. How many songs can you identify? You know the voice of a robin. You know the call of the crow, too, cawing as he flies high over our heads. There is the call of the chickadee. He *tells* you his name.

And those clear, slurred whistles are the song of a meadow lark, perched on a telephone wire in the distance. Look at him through your binoculars. Notice his bright yellow breast with a black line near his throat. See the two white markings on his tail as he flies? He glides to the ground in the meadow. Maybe his nest is there. Learning the names of birds is like making new friends.

Well, here we are, right where Rover and the skunk had their battle. Rover sees us, comes up and wags his tail. He is a friendly dog—except with skunks. As we pet him,

32

we notice that the odor of the skunk is in his fur. The battle was ten days ago, and yet the "perfume" is still there. Even the grass and the ground where the fight took place smell of the combat.

We walk on to the grove of trees. Over there is the decayed log where we first saw Sweet Sue. It looks as if she has been there many times since, because the log is clawed to pieces. Do you think she is somewhere near right now? Let's hide behind those bushes. They will act as a blind for us. Then we can wait patiently for something to happen. We will need a lot of patience if we are to learn more about nature.

We choose our hiding place behind the bushes. Let's make ourselves comfortable in case we have to wait for a while.

"Look! Look! There she is," you exclaim excitedly, pointing to the old stump near the stone wall.

Yes, there she comes. Sweet Sue emerges from the opening between the roots. See how alert she is. She stands motionless at the entrance to her new home.

Listen. There are little squeaking voices somewhere. Sweet Sue is listening to them,

too. Now she turns around and enters the stump. Once more we hear the voices, a whole chorus of them. They come from under the stump. That must be Sweet Sue's home! The sounds are her babies' voices!

Would you like to look into her underground nest?

A few moments pass, and then Sweet Sue comes out again. The voices continue, but she must have decided that nothing serious was wrong with her family. She does not look worried.

She is looking for food. She must have a large amount of food because she must furnish milk for a nest of baby skunks. When she has gone only a few steps, she pounces on a dragonfly and eats it. She goes to the log and scratches about, but she does not find a single grubworm. Probably she has eaten them all on previous visits. She catches a grasshopper, then another and another.

"Is that all she eats?" you ask.

A skunk is not a fussy animal. Sweet Sue will eat almost anything smaller than she is. A few things she likes on her menu are beetles, grasshoppers, cicadas, dragonflies, frogs, toads, lizards, salamanders, crawfish, earthworms, grubworms, mice, rats, gophers, ground squirrels, chipmunks, some kinds of fish, bees, yellow jackets, berries, fungi, eggs, rabbits and sometimes ground nesting birds when young.

Sweet Sue is not the only animal on the scene. Look through your glasses at the tall grass a hundred yards away. There is the beautiful head of a red fox peeping over the grass. He watches Sweet Sue intently but it is not likely that he will attack her. Like all wild creatures, he respects the weapon of the skunk. But he looks as if he would like to take a good bite out of her.

Someone else is watching the skunk. See that small, slender creature standing upright over near the fence? Can you recognize him by his alert manner, his long claws and his striped coat? Yes, it is a gopher. Sweet Sue sees him, too. He is on her list of favorite foods, and she makes a dash toward him. She is quick, but he is quicker. With a squeak of alarm he dives to the safety of his hole.

Sweet Sue finishes her meal of grasshoppers and other bugs, then eats a butterfly as

dessert. Now, with a frog in her mouth, she hurries back to her stump and disappears inside. She cannot stay away from her babies very long. The little ones need to be fed often and they must be kept warm.

Let's move closer because she will not come out again soon. Look at the entrance to the stump. The dirt has been scratched away to enlarge the doorway. The roots through which the opening is made have

been worn smooth because Sweet Sue has gone in and out so often.

"Let's call it Skunk Castle," you say.

Good! I always like to name things. It makes them seem so much more personal. Skunk Castle it shall be.

Then we hear the baby skunk voices again. Hear them? We bend over the doorway. It sounds as if the animals are far back in the ground. There must be a tunnel leading back beyond the stump.

Let's trace the tunnel by sound. We follow it about twelve feet to where there is a pile of round stones, a cave in from the old wall. The voices grow louder. Undoubtedly the home of our friend, Sweet Sue, is underground. This seems like the kind of den a fox would make. It is possible that the fox used it for a season and then went somewhere else. No matter who made it, the den is now the home of Sweet Sue and her family. From

42

the sound we hear, Sweet Sue has a large family.

Do you suppose we would dare dig there?

You shiver as I ask the question. Yet, we are so anxious to see the litter of young, that we decide to try it. If the worst happens, we'll join Rover in the doghouse.

We remove the rocks, one at a time, as quietly and gently as possible. We dig the dirt away with our hands. The voices of the baby animals grow stronger and stronger as the wall grows thinner and thinner. This proves we are digging in the right place. In a way, we almost wish we weren't! Our hearts are beating so loudly that we think the animals can hear them.

What will Sweet Sue think when she knows we are entering her home? What will she do? We do not dare answer our own questions. All we can do now is dig, dig, dig—and hope.

With trembling hands we remove the last stone and make an opening into a dark cave. The voices seem only inches away. We point our flashlight toward the opening and turn the light on.

We gasp with excitement at what we see. There, before us, is a room in the cave which is about two feet square and almost as high. A coating of grasses and leaves covers the floor. Sweet Sue has gathered this material to make her nest.

As our eyes become accustomed to the cave, we are able to see more clearly. There, lying flat on the grass-covered floor, is Sweet Sue. Her eyes are closed, and she looks as if she is fast asleep. Before her, and only a few inches away from us, is a wriggling mass of skunk babies. The mother may think they are beautiful, but we do not! They are such ugly little things that they look as if they are made of rubber. They do not have hair or teeth, their eyes are shut tightly and they do not seem to have ears. It looks as if nature ran out of material when she made baby skunks. See them squirm, and listen to them squeak!

Most of their skin is black, although there are some pink places. But when their hair

comes in, the pink places will have white fur, and the black areas will have black fur.

How many are there? They wiggle so much it is difficult to count them, but we finally decide that there are eight. Few skunk mothers have more than eight babies. There are usually only three or four babies in a family.

Oh, oh! Sweet Sue's nose is starting to twitch. We were so interested in the little family that we forgot we were in an exposed and rather dangerous position. Perhaps Sweet Sue has found our scent. It is not surprising that she does not notice the light we flash in her home. Animals are not disturbed by light as a rule. But if she catches our scent, it will be another matter.

Now she raises her head. It is time for us to leave! Quickly! Replace the rocks and rebuild the wall. Return all the stones and dirt so that her home will be solid.

We chuckle as we hurry away. We have
looked right into the home of a skunk, and
we got away with it. But what could have
happened!

Look back, but keep walking. Sweet Sue is coming out of Skunk Castle, sniffing and looking about to learn what kind of monkey-work is going on around her home. Seeing us, she chatters her teeth. She beats the ground with her feet. She begins to raise her tail. Remember the three warnings? Well, we are wiser than Rover. We heed her warnings, and do not walk; we *run* for distant places!

What a day and what a hike! We will never forget the experience. We will visit Sweet Sue and her family often. It is going to be fun watching her raise her litter. But we will have to be careful. A skunk is never more threatening than when she has young babies.

Now what do we have in our notebook? What have we learned? Here is our list of the things we have noticed about Sweet Sue and her family.

1. Skunk odor lasts a long time after it has been discharged, often for days or weeks.

2. The mother skunk must go out on short, quick hunting trips to get food, so she will have enough milk to feed her young.

3. A skunk eats almost anything that is smaller than he is. Most of the things he eats are pests, although he does kill and eat some birds.

4. While the fox and several other animals could attack the skunk, they seldom do so unless they are desperate for food, for they all are afraid of the skunk's spray.

5. A skunk mother has from three to eight babies. She makes a nest, usually underground, of grass and leaves.

6. The baby skunks are very helpless when they are first born. They have no hair, no teeth, no ears and their eyes are shut tightly.

Our
Third Hike

IT IS a warm spring afternoon. Large clouds drift along lazily in the sky. Nature seems to have "spring fever." Everything is so drowsy. Leaves on the trees scarcely move.

Look at that bird, high, high in the air. See how he sails without flapping his wings. It is a hawk, toying with air currents. Gliding in this manner is his way of resting. He literally sits on the winds and lets them carry him along.

It would be easy for us to be lazy today, too, but we will not. Too many things are happening in nature. What do you suppose is going on down in Sweet Sue's Skunkland? What do you think those eight babies are doing, and how is the mother taking care of her large family?

Get on your walking shoes, and we shall see. This is an active time for skunks. They usually sleep through the middle of the day, and then begin to prowl during the afternoon. Sometimes they prowl all night. Let's go!

Our laziness leaves us when we start hiking. We walk through a meadow, and two cottontail rabbits jump up near our feet and race into the distance. They certainly move fast. No spring fever there!

We walk through an old orchard. An ovenbird sits in a tree and scolds us for being too near his nest which is hidden somewhere in the tall grass. We can always recognize this bird, often called the "teacher bird," for

51

he says plainly, "Teacher! Teacher! Teacher!"

We are nearing Skunkland now. How familiar it has become to us! We pass through the farm. It has a deserted look. The farmer is not there to wave his friendly greeting. Rover is not in his usual place to say "hello" with his wagging tail. The farmer may have taken his family, including Rover, to the village on a shopping trip.

Where is our friend Sweet Sue? We watch the entrance to her home under the old stump, but she does not appear. We search the grove and the hillsides with our eyes, but we still cannot find her. Listen carefully at the place where we found the skunk den. Do you hear the voices of the young skunks? No? Well, what has happened here?

We go down to the little pond. Sweet Sue may have gone there to catch a frog for lunch, but she is not about. Apparently she has not been here, for we do not see her tracks in the sand and mud.

Worried, we wander back toward the farm. Are you concerned? I am. Do you suppose something has happened to the skunk family? Did she move her babies because we dug down into her nest?

We stand in silence and try to answer our own questions. Suddenly, a great commotion breaks the stillness. What a racket! It comes from the direction of the farmer's chicken coop. The door is open. Out comes a flurry of squawking chickens. They run and fly and jump to get as far away from that chicken coop as possible. We run over to see what is causing the trouble.

We peek in the door cautiously, and there in the straw that the farmer has provided for chicken nests, we see our friend Sweet Sue.

"Was she after the chickens?" you ask.

No, it is not likely. Skunks seldom attack

chickens. Look again, and you will see what it is Sweet Sue wants. Note that she is eating the eggs in that nest as quickly as she can. The farmer will not like that, of course. However, the skunk does many things that are good, and the farmer will probably forgive her. But the farmer will be careful to keep his chicken coop door closed in the future.

It is time for us to move a short distance away from the coop and let Sweet Sue come out. If she thought we had her cornered, she would not like it, and we would be sorry. Remember what happened to Rover. We would not enjoy that experience, so we move back a little way.

She moves slowly and deliberately when she comes out through the door. Now we watch something cute! Look closely. The mother skunk wants a drink, and she goes up to the chickens' water dish. Two chickens

come to drink, too. See how they watch Sweet Sue.

The chickens seem to understand that the skunk will not harm them, for they do not fly away. This is not the same situation that we saw in the chicken coop. There, the chickens were confined, and they were afraid. The skunk probably frightened some of them away from their nests. But they are

56

not confined here, and the skunk does not
chase them. When Sweet Sue finishes her
drink, she moves away. Then it is the chickens' turn to drink.

Sweet Sue wanders off through the grass
and searches for food. We watch her from
a distance. We wish skunks were not so fond
of eggs. Stealing and eating eggs is one of
the skunk's few faults. Soon she may come

upon the nest of a pheasant, and eat the eggs just as she did those in the chicken coop. If she frightens a wild duck from its nest, she will have another raw omelette. People would like her so much better if she would stick to a diet of grasshoppers and bugs. But she will not. She likes EGGS!

Suddenly she darts away. She goes over the hill and toward the pond. Quickly! We must keep her in sight. We walk to the top of a ridge, then hide behind trees and bushes. Sweet Sue is standing in a little patch of gravel. A few feet before her is a creature that is not very pretty. It is a snapping turtle, one of nature's really tough creatures.

The gravel patch between the skunk and the turtle tells a story. It shows unmistakable marks of digging and scratching. Now we know what has happened here. That turtle has made a nest in the gravel, and deposited many eggs, perhaps as many as thirty or forty altogether.

Sweet Sue has her own ideas about those eggs, and she waits until the turtle moves on. The turtle will not defend her nest. This animal feels little responsibility about protecting her young. She simply digs a hole, lays her eggs in it, covers them over with gravel and does not return. The heat of the sun hatches the eggs. Sometimes, the eggs do not have a chance to hatch. Many wild wood creatures want those eggs. Raccoons, foxes, coyotes and even dogs like them. But no one likes them more than our friend Sweet Sue. An egg is an egg, she thinks, and it does not make any difference who laid it.

Now watch closely. The turtle goes into the pond. Sweet Sue looks for the exact location of those eggs. Her sensitive nose locates them quickly, and she digs them out. A feast is in store for her! Well, if Sweet Sue must have eggs, it is better for her to eat

turtle eggs. Turtles are not valuable creatures. Because they kill fish and baby ducks,
it does not matter that the eggs never hatch
out into young turtles.

Here is an exciting idea! Do you suppose we could get back to Skunk Castle and have another look at the babies before Sweet Sue returns from her banquet? Let's try it!

We hurry back to the old stump, and listen carefully. Yes, we hear little whimpering voices. The babies are beginning to get hungry and they are chattering about it.

We must work quickly because we may not have much time before the mother returns. She has timed her trips well, for she knows when her babies are hungry. We take away the stones, and dig out the dirt with our hands. The sound of little voices becomes louder.

Excited, we remove the last stone. We point our flashlight inside and turn it on. There they are! All eight of them! They are three weeks old now, and they have fur. See how their stripes are developing? The white line between each skunk's eyes is prominent now, too. They *look* like skunks.

When they see us, they are not at all afraid. One takes a few awkward steps in our direction.

Do you suppose we could reach in and pet one? We reach toward one, and then see something that makes us stop. There is an *extra* skunk edging into the huddle before us, and it is a large one. Sweet Sue has re-

turned, and the look on her face indicates that she wants us to leave.

We do not need a second invitation. Where is that rock? Where is it? We are careless this time, for we feel too sure of ourselves. We do not remember where we placed that all-important stone. Sweet Sue moves toward us just as we find the rock and force it in place. The opening is closed! We do not mind that our fingers are pinched. We must finish the job of building up the wall. Then we must leave!

We run away, pausing only to see Sweet Sue peering out from under the stump. Her expression seems to say, "Now that's enough of that. Don't ever do it again."

She does not need to worry. We will never look in her nest again. Her babies will be large enough to have their own odor sacks soon. If we opened that hole again, nine skunks might turn their odor on us at once.

Who, just who, would want that to happen?
Here is what we have learned.

1. A skunk likes eggs. He will raid a chicken coop to get his favorite food.

2. He also raids the ground nests of wild birds such as pheasant and ducks to get their eggs.

3. He locates and digs up the eggs of turtles and helps keep their population down. Since the turtle destroys young ducks and fish, the skunk is performing a service to man when he eats their eggs.

4. Baby skunks, at three weeks of age, are covered with hair. Their stripes can be seen. They are still in the nest and are fed by the mother, but they are beginning to move around. At this age their eyes are open.

Our
Fourth Hike

A FEELING of summer is in the air as we hike again. The clover and grass make a thick carpet beneath our feet. The trees are heavy with leaves. Daisies in bloom look like fancy fried eggs. Violets smile up from moist places. And hillsides are blue with phlox.

It is fun to meet nature on these hikes. It makes you feel that you have a part in all this interesting drama of the outdoors—and you have!

We take the shortest route to Skunkland, where Sweet Sue and her family live. And

there is the friendly farmer on his mow-
ing machine. He is cutting clover.

See how strong and willing his horses are.
You can tell that the farmer is kind to them.
Maybe they know that this clover is for them.
It will be gathered into the barn. During the
winter when pastures are covered with snow,
it will be part of their food. Then it is called
hay, and the horses love to eat it.

"Have you seen the skunk lately?" we ask
when the farmer comes near.

"Sure have," he answers. "Been around
here a lot. She likes crickets, and there are
lots of them. She caught a field mouse a
while ago and went away carrying it to her
babies. The little fellows have teeth by now
and they need meat along with their milk.
They should be coming out of the nest soon.
Once they start eating meat they are about
ready to leave home and do their own hunting."

Then we must hurry. It would be thrilling to see them come out of that nest the first time. Let's get to our hiding place near Skunk Castle and watch.

Once more we must wait. We crouch back of the bushes and peer anxiously toward the old stump. The entryway shows there has been a lot of coming and going. No doubt Sweet Sue has a hard job. There are eight little stomachs, besides her own, which she must keep full.

By the way, have you wondered why we have not seen the father skunk? It seems he should help feed and care for his family, doesn't it? Well, if he did show up around Skunk Castle, he probably would not be very welcome. Sweet Sue would undoubtedly give him a whipping and chase him away.

You see, skunk fathers do not behave very well. They have a bad habit of eating baby skunks! No wonder mother skunks will not let father skunks come near until the young ones are rather large.

Let's be quiet now. Here she comes! She hurries along through the tall grass, heading for her home. She has something in her mouth. What is it? Look through your field glasses. Now you can see clearly, as she approaches the entrance. She has caught a chipmunk and is bringing it home.

Of course, we do not like her to kill chipmunks, for they are friendly animals. But they are part of her diet, and she helps keep chipmunks and other small animals from becoming too numerous. Anyway, she will not catch many chipmunks. Like gophers, they are too quick. When an enemy comes in sight, they disappear into their underground homes.

Listen! Hear the happy squeals of the babies as she gives them a morsel of food?

But she is coming out already. She must get more food. One chipmunk is simply not enough for eight hungry youngsters.

Come, let's follow her and see what she does next. Keep out of sight the best you can, and do not follow too closely. See that

quick movement as she catches a bug? You did not think she could move so fast, did you? Well, a skunk is very fast when it wants to be.

What is that moving about on the patch of sand toward the pond? It is a long, fat garter snake! Look, the skunk has seen him, or else caught his scent. She rushes to the spot. Now you will see action.

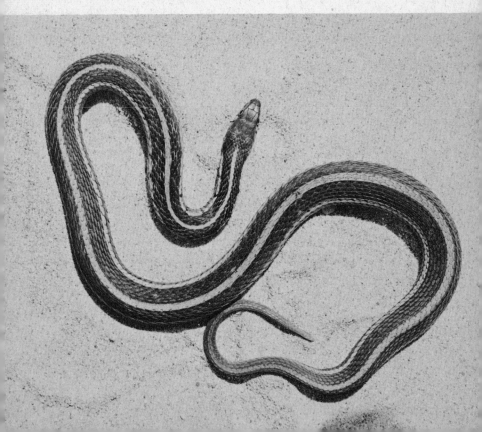

The snake senses danger and moves away. A sudden dash and Sweet Sue has him. Her sharp teeth sink in just behind his head. She shakes him fiercely, and the struggle is over.

With her prize in her mouth she hurries back to her nest. She carries the snake through the doorway.

But look! There is a young one peeking through an opening in the side of the stump.

He wants to know where mother is getting all those delicacies. Maybe this is his first look at the outside world. He seems excited, doesn't he? But he is six weeks old now. It is time for him to think about leaving the underground nursery.

The hard-working mother disappears into the den, and two little heads are thrust out of the doorway. Remember how they looked when we first saw them—before they had any hair, or ears, or their eyes were open?

How they have changed! They are so filled with energy they seem about to burst. They have a good coat of hair now, and their markings are well defined. See the white line between their eyes and the white crown.

Oh, oh! One is coming out. How timid he is! He takes one step at a time and acts as if something were pulling him back. No

doubt that little fellow is breaking the rules. He should not be out alone at his age. The world is full of dangers he does not understand yet.

Hear that shrill cry? It is from a red-shouldered hawk. There he is—in that tree. Focus your glasses on him. He is coming this way. He would like nothing better than a fat, baby skunk for dinner.

Our little friend is in serious trouble, though he does not know it. The sharp talons and fierce beak of the hawk can make mincemeat of him in no time. The huge bird comes on, getting closer and closer. He is within striking distance now.

He spreads his wings for that swift, death-dealing strike for which he is famous. He is not really a bad bird. In nature's scheme, he does much good by feeding on rats and mice and other harmful creatures. But we do not want him to get that cute little skunk!

Something is happening in the den now. There is a lot of commotion inside. Apparently Sweet Sue has discovered that one of her offspring is missing. How she knows, we can only guess. Maybe she has some secret way of counting them in the darkness. Or perhaps she heard the hunting cry of the hawk.

Out the doorway she comes, ready to fight the whole world if necessary. She glances toward the hawk, raising her tail as if to say, "Come on if you want to, and I'll give you something you won't forget as long as you live."

The hawk has no wish to attack Sweet Sue. The little fellow would have been fine, but this other one is much too large. Perhaps the hawk has met a skunk before and recalls what happened.

Sweet Sue is not waiting around for a fight, however. With a quick move, she grabs the young one by the neck and bites hard enough to make him squeal.

Handling him in no gentle manner, she whisks him into Skunk Castle. No hawk would dare enter there. Foiled, the hawk

flies away, and we call after him, "Go get yourself a field mouse. You like them better anyway."

Now from Skunk Castle come pathetic little cries, and we guess that Sweet Sue is teaching her youngsters to behave.

We will leave now and come back early in the morning. Things are happening fast in Skunk Castle, and we do not want to miss anything.

Now let's count over the things we have learned about skunks on our fourth hike:

1. Father skunks are likely to eat baby skunks. So the mother skunks drive the males away during nesting time.

2. When baby skunks get their teeth, at about five or six weeks, they need meat as well as milk. The mother skunk catches small game, such as chipmunks and snakes, for them.

3. While a skunk is usually slow, it can be amazingly quick when catching game.

82

4. Birds of prey, such as the red-shouldered hawk, often catch baby skunks. Thus, mother skunks are careful to keep track of their brood. When a young one is in danger, the mother is fearless in defending it.

5. At six weeks baby skunks have a good coat of fur. They are strong and active, and ready to learn about life in the big outside world.

Our
Fifth Hike

NIGHT still cloaks the world as we set out on this hike. The stars are sparkling beautifully. Do you know how to find the north star? First, locate the Big Dipper. Four stars make up the bowl, and three stars make the handle. It is a large figure and easy to find.

Now, fancy a line between the two stars that make the lower edge of the bowl, opposite the handle. Imagine that this line were drawn through the sky. Imagine that it extended for three times the distance between the two stars. This will bring you near another star, the brightest in that area. It is the North Star.

But it is not the stars that brought us out at this early hour, is it? No, it is Sweet Sue and her family. Something wonderful may happen any time, and we must be there to see it. Any hour Sweet Sue may take her young ones out for their first training in the forest and fields. It will be a thrilling thing to see, and we tingle with excitement.

The first gray streaks of dawn are in the east as we reach our hiding place near Skunk Castle. Stars slowly disappear from the sky. Over at the farm a wakeful rooster crows, and others answer him. Tree toads are calling.

From high in the sky comes the flat, unmusical cry of a bird. Do you recognize it? It could be described as a squawk. A night hawk, you say? That is right! He is a marvelous flyer. He zigzags through the air, feeding on insects and crying in that strange tone.

Now you can see him against that pink cloud. Notice that he works higher and higher, and he circles. Then he does a peculiar thing. He holds his wings in a gliding position and makes a high-speed nose dive toward the earth. Watch, and listen closely.

A short distance above the tree tops he ends his dive, leveling off. Now there is a different sound—almost like the call of a duck. Strangely, that is not a vocal sound. It is made by the rush of air through his feathers as he stops his downward plunge. Now he takes up his zigzagging flight once more, gathering insects, and working his way upward. When he is high enough, he will execute that dive again.

The morning light grows stronger, and the world about us takes form. We can make out Skunk Castle. A silent, dark form moves along the ground and enters it. Sweet Sue has been out on a hunting trip and is returning. No doubt she has some article of food for her family. Will she take her family out now? No one can answer but Sweet Sue, and she just lets us guess.

Full daylight comes, and still all is quiet at Skunk Castle. We watch and watch until our eyes grow tired. We remain quiet, however, using all the patience we have. Sweet Sue must bring those youngsters out soon. They are six weeks old now. By the time they are eight or nine weeks old, their training will be finished and they will be out in the world on their own.

Our hope fades as the hours drag by. Midday is when skunks like to rest. Sweet Sue probably has her family all cuddled up in a woolly pile back in the den. We wait on.

At noon we eat some sandwiches we brought in our pockets, but our eyes never stray from the doorway in that old stump.

"All things come to him who waits." It is late afternoon, and we begin to doubt that this saying is true. But suddenly, without hesitation or timidity, Sweet Sue comes walking out. Then comes that thrilling sight for which we have been watching! Eight cute and cunning little skunklets trail behind her.

You ask, "How do the little ones know they are to come out now?"

No one can answer that question. Sweet Sue has come and gone through that doorway scores and scores of times. The young ones watched her and made no effort to follow. Now they are to follow and they know it. Somehow, she has told them. That is sure. But how, she alone knows.

See how jaunty and fearless they are! They have perfect confidence in their "weapon." Even at their tender age they are fully armed. Woe unto anything that attacks!

Notice the difference in their markings. Several have full-length stripes like their mother. One has only the mark on his head and the start of a stripe. Still another has one long stripe and a short one. Some have a white tip on their tail. Some do not.

Now, let's keep as close to them as we can without frightening them.

Fortunately for us, the skunk is not worried by every sound or movement. We may stay a short distance away, watching from behind the trees and bushes. This is serious business to our skunk family. The little ones are being trained in what they must do to survive in the big world they have entered. There is no time for play.

Sweet Sue teaches them by example. She catches a cricket. One of the babies comes up to get it, but she keeps it away from him. From this day on, if he wants food he must catch it for himself. This he does, and so do the others. Through the grass they go, gathering a harvest of bugs.

Sweet Sue shows them about the old log, and they all dig in it. A few grubs are their reward. She shows them some plants that are good for food. Then she leads them into a patch of wild strawberries on the hillside. See how they go after those berries! Later they will find raspberries and blackberries to add to their diet.

Now one little fellow who has full length stripes discovers a snake. He is wild with excitement. From a few feet away Sweet Sue watches the youngster. Though he has never battled a snake before, he knows just where to strike it. "How does he know," you ask? Well, that kind of knowing we call *instinct*. The snake is dead quickly, and the young hunter makes the most of his meal.

Sweet Sue leads her litter on. Sometimes they are in a long straight line. Sometimes they are everywhere. How quickly they learn what to do and how to do it. At first, grasshoppers are too fast for them and get away. But the youngsters learn to pounce suddenly on the hopping creatures, and they seem very fond of eating them.

We observe an interesting thing about this family. There is some kind of silent talk between the mother and the young. See how they are scattered, each tending to his own little problem? The mother is with them most of the time. Yet sometimes she disappears into the grass or brush. They make no attempt to follow her. They seem to know she will return.

But presently she wants the family to move on. She walks away as she has done many times before. Yet this time they all leave what they are doing and follow her! She has made them understand that it is time to go on to other food and other adventures.

Now Sweet Sue leads her family, and us, toward the little pond. Here, in a shallow pool, are three frogs sunning themselves. Watch the babies. This is a kind of food the mother has often brought to the nest. Will they recognize it, and can they catch those quick jumping creatures before they get to deep water?

Once more we see the marvelous quickness of the skunk. Sweet Sue does not need to show them how. Two of them pounce on one frog and drag him out of the water. The other two frogs, frightened and bewildered, jump right toward the skunks. Sweet Sue catches one, and the youngsters catch the

other. There is a sharp scuffle among the skunks to decide just who gets the delicate dinner. Finally, everyone gets some.

How long will the hunting lesson last? If the skunks are as tired as we are, it will be over soon. But Sweet Sue has more things to teach her brood before they return to the nest. See? She is leading them into the meadow. They have found a nest of field mice. What excitement! The mice run and jump for their lives, and the young skunks go right after them. It looks as if the skunks are having more fun than ever. They go jumping and running about, even after the last mouse is caught.

Sweet Sue has a definite purpose in mind. She leads her family across the meadow.

The baby skunks follow obediently. Sweet Sue heads directly for a place where a dozen beehives are on the ground. These hives belong to our farmer friend, and here the bees make lots of honey for him.

What is Sweet Sue going to do there? Watch through your glasses, for we would not want to be too close if those bees get angry.

The family of skunks go up to the very entrances of the hives. Now, could you believe that if you did not see it yourself? The bees swarm about them, but Sweet Sue and her family are unconcerned. See, they are catching the bees and eating them!

How can they do that and not be stung? They know the trick, and the nine skunks account for a great number of bees. The farmer is not going to like that. Eating bees is another fault of the skunks, for bees are valuable.

98

At this moment, something happens to bring the first hunting lesson to an end. Out on the still evening air comes the voice of an owl. Sweet Sue shows immediate concern. She gives a note of alarm, and her family comes to her.

The voice is like that of the great horned owl, her worst enemy. No wonder Sweet Sue is concerned.

The voice comes from a tree. But the owl is very hard to see because he blends so well into the forest background. Can you see him, if you look closely?

Sweet Sue goes straight for the grove and Skunk Castle. She passes very close to us and does not notice us. The weird call comes again. The skunk parade increases its speed. Into the den they go; Sweet Sue is the last one in.

The voice comes from a tree again. Sweet Sue does not know it, but this is not the great

horned owl. It is the long-eared owl. He is
much smaller and not so dangerous to animals like the skunk.

Sweet Sue and her family will not come
out for a while. To hear an owl is a very

frightening thing for them, and they will stay in until danger is past. We are glad to go home, too, for Sweet Sue has worn us out on this first hunting lesson.

We leave Sweet Sue and her family to recover from their fright.

This has been a grand hike, and we have learned many things about the skunk. We shall list them.

1. When young skunks are about six weeks old, they are ready to leave their dens and go on training trips under the guidance of their mother.

2. The mother skunk shows her young how to catch bugs, grasshoppers, mice and small snakes.

3. Like many other animals, the skunk mother has a silent method of talking to her babies to make them obey her.

4. Skunks catch and eat live bees, including the stingers.

5. When the training time comes, baby skunks are prepared to use their odor weapon.

6. Not all striped skunks are marked the same. Some have white at the head and no stripes. Others have two long stripes, which may run from the head to the end of the tail. Some have a white tip on the tail, while others do not. But all of them have the white stripe between their eyes.

7. The great horned owl is the skunk's worst enemy. The huge bird does not mind the odor of the skunk, and will attack even a full-grown animal.

Our
Sixth Hike

THREE WEEKS have slipped by since we saw Sweet Sue and her family on that first hunting trip. Will you ever forget how cute they were? Remember how they chased bugs and mice and the way they scampered home when the owl called?

Though we were not there to see it, Sweet Sue probably took her litter hunting many times after that first adventure. She had many things to teach them. They learned to get food, to find a home, to defend themselves and to know their friends and enemies in nature. This training went on day and night.

Each skunklet was being prepared to make his way in the world.

Now we are anxious to go on another hike. We shall hike out to Skunkland and see what else we can learn about these interesting animals.

Notice that summer has come to our fields and groves. The wheat, oats and corn are growing high. Wild roses bloom on the hillsides, and other flowers make a colorful carpet in the meadows.

We have a strange feeling as we approach Skunk Castle. The old stump and den seem deserted. Wind and rain have filled the doorway with sand. There are no animal tracks to be seen. Surely no creature has gone in or out of the doorway recently. Shall we look into the den?

We begin to remove the rocks. Do you feel a little nervous about doing this? I do. True, at the doorway it looked as if no animal had entered for days. But suppose the skunks have made a new entrance and are inside? Better be ready to leave in a hurry!

We reach the last rock. Then we sit for several minutes and wonder what will happen to us. It is quite still inside the den, but skunks are capable of being very quiet.

Then our courage returns, and we remove the stone. We flash our light into the den. No living creature is there. We are greeted with emptiness.

The wall has caved in slightly and partly covers the bed of leaves and grass. It is a deserted home, and the sight of it leaves us with a feeling of loneliness. Those skunks were our friends, and we feel an interest in them.

We search over the hillside and down by the pond. No skunks. We call Sweet Sue, forgetting that she does not know the name we gave her.

Come. We will ask the farmer if he knows anything about the animals. He is plowing in the corn field with a tractor. He halts his machine and shuts off the engine so he can talk to us. "The baby skunks?" he says, in answer to our question. "Oh, they grew up. They're scattered all over the country by now. Have to scatter, you know. Wouldn't be enough food for them if they all stayed in one place."

With a feeling of regret, we ask about the mother skunk. Has he seen her? Is she all right?

"Yes," he says, with a laugh. "She moved in on us. Stays under the barn. She gets along fine with the animals. You might see her over there. Be careful though. A big male skunk comes to see her occasionally, and he isn't so friendly. I'm glad to have them around. They do a lot of good on the farm."

108

We ask him if the animals eat chicken eggs and kill his honeybees.

"Yes, they would," he says, mopping his brow. "But I put up wire around the chicken house, and I put my beehives on a platform four feet off the ground. They are out of the skunks' reach. A skunk can't climb, you know. They pay me for my trouble by killing rats, mice, worms and bugs."

We walk over to the farm buildings and look around carefully. Yes, there is a skunk near that fence—but it is not Sweet Sue!

See how large it is, and notice the white tail! Sweet Sue has a black tail. That big fellow is not friendly, either. Look at him disappear into the hedge at the sight of us! This is the large male skunk the farmer told us about. He is probably Sweet Sue's mate.

We go over to the barn. Our farmer friend told us Sweet Sue is living under this building. There is a hole leading under the foundation, and there are skunk tracks here. That is the entrance to her new home.

The barn door is open. We look in and see a pony. He is watching something near his front feet where there is a rustle in the straw. We look closely, and there is Sweet Sue!

Remember, the farmer said the skunk and the farm animals were friends. But look out! Sweet Sue is coming our way. Get behind that shed and watch!

Here she comes! She is a large and beau-

111

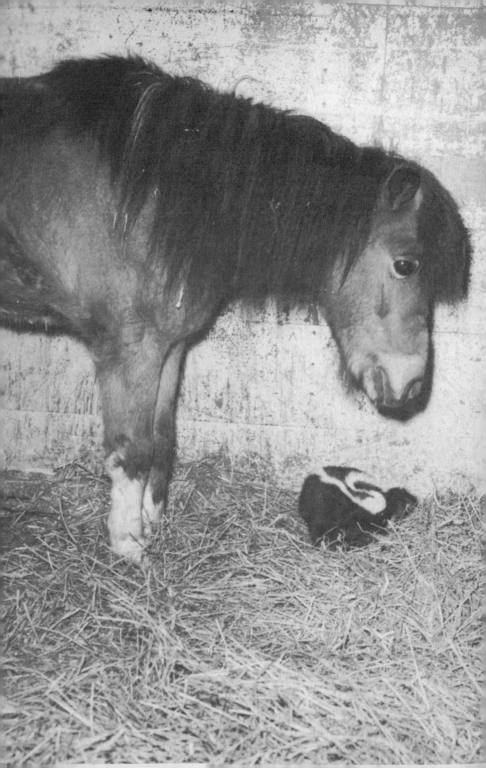

tiful animal, and it seems that her fur is thicker than when we last saw her. She is fatter, too, so she is getting enough to eat. Now that the responsibility of raising her family is over, she is gaining weight and taking life easy.

As she comes out the door, she runs right into the farm cat. What will happen now? Will the cat have the same experience Rover had?

No, apparently they understand each

other. Sweet Sue does not even give a warning signal. She pokes her nose at the cat in a friendly greeting. The cat playfully touches Sweet Sue's nose with her paw.

Then Sweet Sue ambles on. She walks among the cattle and horses without fear. They do not notice her. She comes upon a dish of food put out for the chickens. She helps herself to more than her share. Although the chickens might not like it, they do not object.

Then Sweet Sue goes on down a lane toward the place where we saw the big male skunk, and disappears into the hedge. Maybe they "have a date."

We turn our steps homeward now. Our hike is just about over. We look back on the endless acres of fields, pastures, orchards and groves. Somewhere out there, are eight skunks we knew as babies. What will happen to them? Not all of them will survive.

One or more may fall victim to great horned owls, foxes, coyotes, wolves or even dogs. Sometimes these animals grow so desperately hungry that they will brave the spray of a skunk. The skunks which do survive will grow fatter and fatter as the season goes on.

But the most terrible danger our skunks must face is the steel trap. Trappers place these cruel steel jaws where skunks live. After the hunter has dried the skins, he sells them to companies that deal in furs. Here, again, the skunk serves mankind. His hide, with its pretty fur, will be used to make coats or to trim them.

Not all of our skunks will be caught that way. Those which escape will live on through the autumn. When winter comes, the animals will sleep most of the time. Some of them may return to Skunk Castle. Often a number of them den up together to keep warm.

It would be nice if Sweet Sue and her babies huddled up together for the winter. It is possible. However, when next spring comes, they will scatter far and wide, and each will find a home of his own.

Sweet Sue may keep Skunk Castle for her own then. When next April comes, there may be more babies, and our story could start all over again.

Did you ever hear this poem?

"A skunk sat on a stump.
The skunk said the stump stunk;
The stump said the skunk stunk."

Say it again. Say it several times rapidly, if you can! Now, what have we learned on our sixth hike?

1. As soon as a mother skunk has trained her little ones in the art of hunting, they go hunting independently.

2. The animals may desert their home in late summer and wander about the countryside.

3. Skunks may become friendly with farm animals and get along peacefully with them.

4. Farmers may prevent skunks from eating chicken eggs by properly fencing in the chicken yard. They save bees from skunks by putting the hives on platforms four feet or more off the ground. Skunks cannot climb.

5. After baby skunks are able to take care of themselves, male skunks may return to the family.

6. The worst danger skunks face is the hunter's steel trap. Many skunks are caught and killed this way every year. Trappers sell the skunk hides to be made into coats and as trimming for other garments.

7. Other enemies which kill skunks are the great horned owl, foxes, coyotes, wolves or dogs. However, these predatory animals must be very hungry before they will risk the spray of a skunk and attack him.

8. Skunks sleep most of the winter. A number of them may sleep in the same den in order to keep warm.

9. Our hikes have been great fun, and we are going to do more of them in the future. We will learn more about the great world of nature.